Ladybird Readers

Sports Day

Series Editor: Sorrel Pitts
Text adapted by Coleen Degnan-Veness

LADYBIRD BOOKS

UK | USA | Canada | Ireland | Australia
India | New Zealand | South Africa

Ladybird Books is part of the Penguin Random House group of companies
whose addresses can be found at global.penguinrandomhouse.com.
www.penguin.co.uk   www.puffin.co.uk   www.ladybird.co.uk

Text adapted from Peppa Pig: Sports Day, first published by Ladybird Books, 2008
This version first published by Ladybird Books, 2016
005

Illustrations © 2003 ABD Ltd/Ent/ One UK Ltd/Hasbro
Text © 2016 ABD Ltd/Ent. One UK Ltd/Hasbro

Licensed by

Printed in China

The authorized representative in the EEA is Penguin Random House Ireland,
Morrison Chambers, 32 Nassau Street, Dublin D02 YH68

A CIP catalogue record for this book is available from the British Library

ISBN: 978-0-241-26222-1

All correspondence to:
Ladybird Books
Penguin Random House Children's
One Embassy Gardens, 8 Viaduct Gardens, London SW11 7BW

MIX
Paper from
responsible sources
FSC® C018179

Sports Day

Based on the Peppa Pig
TV series

Picture words

Emily Elephant

Peppa

George

Madame Gazelle

Daddy Pig

Richard Rabbit

Rebecca Rabbit

baton

pull

race

rope

It was Sports Day at school.

Peppa, George, and all their friends were there.

The first game was a race.
The friends had to run fast.

"One, two, three—go!" said
Madame Gazelle.

They ran very fast!

But Peppa started slowly.

She did not come first and she was not happy.

Rebecca Rabbit came
first in the race.

"Well done!" said all
her friends.

13

In the second game,
the friends had to make
a long jump.

"One, two, three—go!" said Madame Gazelle again.

But George's jump was
not long and he did not
come first.

George was
not happy.

Richard Rabbit came first.
"Well done!" said all
his friends.

In the third game, the moms and dads had to run to their child. They had to give them a baton.

"One, two, three—go!" said Madame Gazelle again.

Daddy Pig ran very fast with his baton.

"Here, Peppa!" said Daddy Pig. He gave her the baton. "Run fast!"

But Peppa did not run
very fast.

Emily Elephant came first.

"Well done!" said all
her friends.

Peppa did not come first
and she was not happy.

Sports Day finished with a game for all the boys and girls. They had to pull a long rope.

"One, two, three—go!" said Madame Gazelle.

The boys wanted to come first. The girls wanted to come first, too.

The boys were very strong AND the girls were very strong. But the rope was not strong!

"The boys came first AND the girls came first!" said Madame Gazelle.

"Great!" said Peppa. "I came first! I like Sports Day!"

Activities

The key below describes the skills practiced in each activity.

Spelling and writing

Reading

Speaking

Critical thinking

Preparation for the Cambridge Young Learners Exams

1 Look and read.
Put a or a in the box.

1  This is Daddy Pig.

2   This is Richard Rabbit. □

3  This is Rebecca Rabbit. □

4  This is Madame Gazelle. □

5  This is George. □

2 Look and read. Write yes or no.

It was Sports Day at school.
Peppa, George, and all their friends were there.

The first game was a race.
The friends had to run fast.

"One, two, three—go!" said Madame Gazelle.

They ran very fast!

1 It was Sports Day at school.

...... yes ......

2 The first game was a long jump.

....

3 The friends had to walk fast.

....

3 Look and read. Choose the correct word and write it on the line. 📖 ✏️ ⬢

| baton | pull | race | rope |

1 People run fast, but only one person comes first.

_____race_____

2 Daddy Pig gave this to Peppa.

_____

3 The children pull this on Sports Day.

_____

4 People do this with their hands.

_____

4 **Work with a friend.**
Look at the two pictures.
How are they different?

a

"Here, Peppa!" said
Daddy Pig. He gave her
the baton. "Run fast!"

But Peppa did not run
very fast.

b

The first game was a race.
The friends had to run fast.

"One, two, three—go!" said
Madame Gazelle.

They ran very fast!

*In picture a, they
are running.*

*In picture b, they are
not running.*

5 Match the two parts of the sentence.

The first game was a race.
The friends had to run fast.

"One, two, three--go!" said Madame Gazelle.

They ran very fast!

1 Peppa was in the first race, but

2 Peppa

3 Daddy Pig gave

4 Peppa and her friends had to

a started slowly.

b run fast.

c George was not.

d Peppa the baton.

6 Look at the letters. Write the words.

1 t s S p o r

2 c e r a

3 l y w o l s

4 f t r s i

1 It was ___Sports___ Day at school.

2 Daddy Pig watched Peppa in the

_____ .

3 Peppa wanted to come first, but she

started _____ .

4 Peppa did not come

_____ .

7 Look and read. Write the answers.

Rebecca Rabbit came first in the race.

"Well done!" said all her friends.

1 Who came first in the race?

Rebecca Rabbit

2 Who said, "Well done!"?

3 What color was Rebecca's mommy's dress?

8 **Work with a friend. Look at the pictures and tell the story.**

Example:

> *Peppa, George, Mommy Pig, and Daddy Pig went to Sports Day . . .*

9 **Look and read. Write the correct words on the lines.** 📖 ✏️ ✿

Rebecca Rabbit came first in the race.

"Well done!" said all her friends.

came
done
first
happy
started

In the ¹ _first_ race, the friends

ran fast. But Peppa ² _____

slowly. She did not come first.

She was not ³ _____ .

Rebecca Rabbit ⁴ _____ first.

"Well ⁵ _____ !" said all

her friends.

10 Circle the correct words.

In the second game, the friends had to make a long jump.

"One, two, three—go!" said Madame Gazelle again.

1 In the second game, the friends had to make a long

   a run.

   b jump.

2 "One, two, three—go!" said Madame

   a Elephant.

   b Gazelle.

3 But George's jump was not

   a long.

   b fast.

11 Read the text. Write the right words on the lines. 📖 ✏️ ⭐

1	bad	easy	good
2	Don't worry!	Well done!	Oh dear!
3	had to	have to	has to
4	running	ran	run

George was not ¹ _good_ at the long jump. Richard Rabbit came first. " ² _____ " said all his friends. In the third game, the moms and dads ³ _____ run to their child. Daddy Pig

⁴ _____ very fast with his baton.

12 Work with a friend. One of the three pictures is different. How is it different?

1

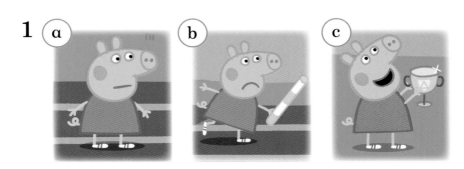

Example:

Picture c is different because Peppa is happy.

2

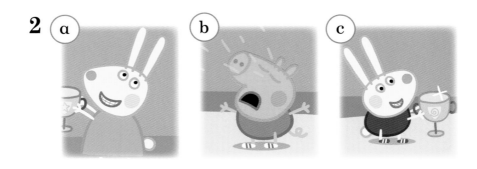

13 Write the correct words.

baton   Here   third

"Here, Peppa!" said Daddy Pig. He gave her the baton. "Run fast!"

But Peppa did not run very fast.

1 The ___third___ game was the baton race.

2 Daddy Pig ran very fast with his

_____ .

3 "_____ , Peppa! Run fast!" said Daddy Pig.

14 Circle the correct words.

Emily Elephant came first.

"Well done!" said all her friends.

Peppa did not come first and she was not happy.

1 Emily Elephant came first in the

   a baton race.

   b long jump.

2 Peppa's baton was

   a red and white.

   b yellow and white.

3 Emily Elephant's baton was

   a orange and white.

   b purple and white.

15 **Look and read. Choose the correct words and write them on the lines.** 📖 ✏️

long
jump

running
race

Sports
Day

baton
race

1 Peppa, George, and their friends were
  at _____Sports Day_____.

2 Rebecca Rabbit was good at the

  _____.

3 Richard Rabbit was good at the

  _____.

4 Daddy Pig was good at the

  _____.

16 Ask and answer the questions with a friend.

1
> Do you like Sports Day?

> Yes, I like Sports Day.

2 What Sports Day game is your favorite?

3 Do you like coming first?

4 Do your mommy and daddy come to your Sports Day?

17 **Circle the correct words.**

1 Peppa: "Did you win the running race?"

Emily: **a** "No, I did not."

   b "No, I cannot."

2 Friends: "Well done, Rebecca!"

Rebecca: **a** "No!"

   b "Thank you!"

3 Daddy Pig: "Can you run fast, Peppa?"

Peppa: **a** "Me too!"

   b "Yes, I can."

4 Daddy Pig: "Why are you sad, Peppa?"

Peppa: **a** "Because I did not come first."

   b "Because I had to make a long jump."

Level 2

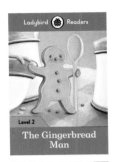

The Gingerbread Man

978–0–241–25442–4 ☐

Sly Fox and Red Hen

978–0–241–25443–1 ☐

The Monster Next Door

978–0–241–25444–8 ☐

Wild Animals

978–0–241–25445–5 ☐

Little Red Riding Hood

978–0–241–25446–2 ☐

Dinosaurs

978–0–241–25447–9 ☐

Topsy and Tim The Big Race

978–0–241–25448–6 ☐

Peter Rabbit Goes to the Treehouse

978–0–241–25449–3 ☐

Sports Day

978–0–241–26222–1 ☐

Going on a Picnic

978–0–241–26221–4 ☐

Now you're ready for Level 3!

Notes
CEFR levels are based on guidelines set out in the Council of Europe's European Framework. Cambridge Young Learners English (YLE) Exams give a reliable indication of a child's progression in learning English.